READING AND WRITING HANDBOOKS

1000
INSTANT WORDS

W9-CMN-025

EDWARD FRY, PH.D.

CB

CONTEMPORARY BOOKS

a division of NTC/CONTEMPORARY PUBLISHING GROUP
Lincolnwood, Illinois USA

ISBN: 0-8092-0880-6

Published by Contemporary Books,
a division of NTC/Contemporary Publishing Group, Inc.,
4255 West Touhy Avenue,
Lincolnwood (Chicago), Illinois 60712-1975 U.S.A.

0 1 2 3 4 5 6 7 8 9   VL   12 11 10 9 8 7 6 5 4

Market Development Manager
Noreen Lopez

Editorial Director
Cynthia Krejcsi

Project Editor
Christine Kelner

Production
Thomas D. Scharf

Cover and Interior Design
Kristy Sheldon

CONTENTS

INTRODUCTION

A list of high-frequency words is a scientifically determined list of the most commonly used words in the English language. It is indeed a basic "tool" for reading and writing teachers, literacy tutors, curriculum developers, researchers, and authors of children's books.

The core of this book is 1000 Instant Words (sight words) ranked in order of frequency, with the most common words first. These 1000 words are arranged in groups of five words to indicate to the teacher that not many should be taught at one time. This rank order list is also a suggested teaching order in which beginning readers or writers normally learn new basic words while they learn many other terms, such as names or subject words.

This section is followed by the same 1000 words arranged in alphabetical order for ease in looking up the position of any word. The list is based on the *American Heritage Dictionary* five-million-word count but with a different ranking, since variant word forms were combined and later reranked.

The next section shows how to test students in order to start teaching the Instant Words at an appropriate place. It will help teachers select words to teach those who have limited reading or writing ability.

Next, there are several suggestions for teaching the Instant Words with games, flash cards, reading practice, and spelling lessons.

The final section consists of 100 picture nouns. These everyday words are a helpful addition to the Instant Words because new readers can use them early on to read and write more meaningful sentences. The picture nouns may also appeal to students who learn reading and writing best by using concrete or easily visualized words.

Beginning readers, whose ability ranges from none to the upper-fifth-grade equivalency level, need to master a high-frequency vocabulary such as the Instant Words. For example, they should be able to read the first 300 of these words "instantly"—without a moment's hesitation—because these words make up 65 percent of all written material. In fact, more than half of the text of every newspaper article, textbook, children's story, and novel is composed of just these 300 words. It is virtually impossible for students to concentrate on comprehension if they are stuck on a word such as *their*.

Another problem is that some of these high-frequency words do not follow phonics rules. For example, how does a student readily sound out *of* or *said?* The answer is that beginning readers need to learn these words as "sight words," learning to recognize these common words as they read them.

RANK ORDER 1–30 _____

1–5

the
of
and
a
to

6–10

in
is
you
that
it

11–15

he
was
for
on
are

16–20

as
with
his
they
I

21–25

at
be
this
have
from

26–30

or
one
had
by
word

Rank Order 31–60

31–35

but
not
what
all
were

36–40

we
when
your
can
said

41–45

there
use
an
each
which

46–50

she
do
how
their
if

51–55

will
up
other
about
out

56–60

many
then
them
these
so

RANK ORDER 61–90

61–65

some
her
would
make
like

66–70

him
into
time
has
look

71–75

two
more
write
go
see

76–80

number
no
way
could
people

81–85

my
than
first
water
been

86–90

call
who
oil
now
find

RANK ORDER 91–120

91–95

long
down
day
did
get

96–100

come
made
may
part
over

101–105

new
sound
take
only
little

106–110

work
know
place
year
live

111–115

me
back
give
most
very

116–120

after
thing
our
just
name

121–125

good
sentence
man
think
say

136–140

old
any
same
tell
boy

126–130

great
where
help
through
much

141–145

follow
came
want
show
also

131–135

before
line
right
too
mean

146–150

around
form
three
small
set

RANK ORDER 151–180

151–155

put
end
does
another
well

156–160

large
must
big
even
such

161–165

because
turn
here
why
ask

166–170

went
men
read
need
land

171–175

different
home
us
move
try

176–180

kind
hand
picture
again
change

181–185

off
play
spell
air
away

186–190

animal
house
point
page
letter

191–195

mother
answer
found
study
still

196–200

learn
should
America
world
high

201–205

every
near
add
food
between

206–210

own
below
country
plant
last

211–215

school
father
keep
tree
never

216–220

start
city
earth
eye
light

221–225

thought
head
under
story
saw

226–230

left
don't
few
while
along

231–235

might
close
something
seem
next

236–240

hard
open
example
begin
life

241–245

always
those
both
paper
together

246–250

got
group
often
run
important

251–255

until
children
side
feet
car

256–260

mile
night
walk
white
sea

261–265

began
grow
took
river
four

266–270

carry
state
once
book
hear

271–275

stop
without
second
late
miss

286–290

above
girl
sometimes
mountain
cut

276–280

idea
enough
eat
face
watch

291–295

young
talk
soon
list
song

281–285

far
Indian
real
almost
let

296–300

being
leave
family
it's
afternoon

301–305

body
music
color
stand
sun

306–310

questions
fish
area
mark
dog

311–315

horse
birds
problem
complete
room

316–320

knew
since
ever
piece
told

321–325

usually
didn't
friends
easy
heard

326–330

order
red
door
sure
become

331–335

top
ship
across
today
during

346–350

measure
remember
early
waves
reached

336–340

short
better
best
however
low

351–355

listen
wind
rock
space
covered

341–345

hours
black
products
happened
whole

356–360

fast
several
hold
himself
toward

361–365

five
step
morning
passed
vowel

366–370

true
hundred
against
pattern
numeral

371–375

table
north
slowly
money
map

376–380

farm
pulled
draw
voice
seen

381–385

cold
cried
plan
notice
south

386–390

sing
war
ground
fall
king

391–395

town
I'll
unit
figure
certain

396–400

field
travel
wood
fire
upon

401–405

done
English
road
half
ten

406–410

fly
gave
box
finally
wait

411–415

correct
oh
quickly
person
became

416–420

shown
minutes
strong
verb
stars

421–425

front
feel
fact
inches
street

426–430

decided
contain
course
surface
produce

431–435

building
ocean
class
note
nothing

436–440

rest
carefully
scientists
inside
wheels

441–445

stay
green
known
island
week

446–450

less
machine
base
ago
stood

451–455

plane
system
behind
ran
round

456–460

boat
game
force
brought
understand

461–465

warm
common
bring
explain
dry

466–470

though
language
shape
deep
thousands

471–475

yes
clear
equation
yet
government

476–480

filled
heat
full
hot
check

481–485

object
am
rule
among
noun

486–490

power
cannot
able
six
size

491–495

dark
ball
material
special
heavy

496–500

fine
pair
circle
include
built

501–505

can't
matter
square
syllables
perhaps

506–510

bill
felt
suddenly
test
direction

511–515

center
farmers
ready
anything
divided

516–520

general
energy
subject
Europe
moon

521–525

region
return
believe
dance
members

526–530

picked
simple
cells
paint
mind

531–535

love
cause
rain
exercise
eggs

536–540

train
blue
wish
drop
developed

541–545

window
difference
distance
heart
sit

546–550

sum
summer
wall
forest
probably

551–555

legs
sat
main
winter
wide

556–560

written
length
reason
kept
interest

561–565

arms
brother
race
present
beautiful

566–570

store
job
edge
past
sign

571–575

record
finished
discovered
wild
happy

576–580

beside
gone
sky
glass
million

581–585

west
lay
weather
root
instruments

586–590

meet
third
months
paragraph
raised

591–595

represent
soft
whether
clothes
flowers

596–600

shall
teacher
held
describe
drive

601–605

cross
speak
solve
appear
metal

616–620

care
floor
hill
pushed
baby

606–610

son
either
ice
sleep
village

621–625

buy
century
outside
everything
tall

611–615

factors
result
jumped
snow
ride

626–630

already
instead
phrase
soil
bed

631–635

copy
free
hope
spring
case

646–650

section
lake
consonant
within
dictionary

636–640

laughed
nation
quite
type
themselves

651–655

hair
age
amount
scale
pounds

641–645

temperature
bright
lead
everyone
method

656–660

although
per
broken
moment
tiny

661–665

possible
gold
milk
quiet
natural

666–670

lot
stone
act
build
middle

671–675

speed
count
cat
someone
sail

676–680

rolled
bear
wonder
smiled
angle

681–685

fraction
Africa
killed
melody
bottom

686–690

trip
hole
poor
let's
fight

691–695

surprise
French
died
beat
exactly

696–700

remain
dress
iron
couldn't
fingers

701–705

row
least
catch
climbed
wrote

706–710

shouted
continued
itself
else
plains

711–715

gas
England
burning
design
joined

716–720

foot
law
ears
grass
you're

721–725

grew
skin
valley
cents
key

726–730

president
brown
trouble
cool
cloud

731–735

lost
sent
symbols
wear
bad

736–740

save
experiment
engine
alone
drawing

741–745

east
pay
single
touch
information

746–750

express
mouth
yard
equal
decimal

751–755

yourself
control
practice
report
straight

766–770

wire
choose
clean
visit
bit

756–760

rise
statement
stick
party
seeds

771–775

whose
received
garden
please
strange

761–765

suppose
woman
coast
bank
period

776–780

caught
fell
team
God
captain

781–785

direct
ring
serve
child
desert

786–790

increase
history
cost
maybe
business

791–795

separate
break
uncle
hunting
flow

796–800

lady
students
human
art
feeling

801–805

supply
corner
electric
insects
crops

806–810

tone
hit
sand
doctor
provide

811–815

thus
won't
cook
bones
tail

816–820

board
modern
compound
mine
wasn't

821–825

fit
addition
belong
safe
soldiers

826–830

guess
silent
trade
rather
compare

831–835

crowd
poem
enjoy
elements
indicate

836–840

except
expect
flat
seven
interesting

841–845

sense
string
blow
famous
value

856–860

fun
loud
consider
suggested
thin

846–850

wings
movement
pole
exciting
branches

861–865

position
entered
fruit
tied
rich

851–855

thick
blood
lie
spot
bell

866–870

dollars
send
sight
chief
Japanese

871–875

stream
planets
rhythm
eight
science

876–880

major
observe
tube
necessary
weight

881–885

meat
lifted
process
army
hat

886–890

property
particular
swim
terms
current

891–895

park
sell
shoulder
industry
wash

896–900

block
spread
cattle
wife
sharp

901–905

company
radio
we'll
action
capital

906–910

factories
settled
yellow
isn't
southern

911–915

truck
fair
printed
wouldn't
ahead

916–920

chance
born
level
triangle
molecules

921–925

France
repeated
column
western
church

926–930

sister
oxygen
plural
various
agreed

931–935

opposite
wrong
chart
prepared
pretty

936–940

solution
fresh
shop
suffix
especially

941–945

shoes
actually
nose
afraid
dead

946–950

sugar
adjective
fig
office
huge

951–955

gun
similar
death
score
forward

956–960

stretched
experience
rose
allow
fear

961–965

workers
Washington
Greek
women
bought

966–970

led
march
northern
create
British

971–975

difficult
match
win
doesn't
steel

976–980

total
deal
determine
evening
nor

981–985

rope
cotton
apple
details
entire

986–990

corn
substances
smell
tools
conditions

RANK ORDER 991–1000 _____

991–995

cows
track
arrived
located
sir

996–1000

seat
division
effect
underline
view

SIGNS AS SIGHT WORDS _____

The words on these common signs are important for students to learn as sight words.

NO TURN ON RED

 DO NOT ENTER

DO NOT PASS

SPEED LIMIT 55

 WRONG WAY

 ONE WAY

 DETOUR

 Telephone

 YIELD

  NO LEFT TURN

 LANE CLOSED

 DANGER

 FIRE HOSE

 EXIT

 POISON

Word	#	Word	#	Word	#	Word	#	Word	#
a	4	because	161	catch	703	day	93	equal	749
able	488	become	330	cattle	898	dead	945	equation	473
about	54	bed	630	caught	776	deal	977	especially	940
above	286	been	85	cause	532	death	953	Europe	519
across	333	before	131	cells	528	decided	426	even	159
act	668	began	261	center	511	decimal	750	evening	979
action	904	begin	239	cents	724	deep	469	ever	318
actually	942	behind	453	century	622	describe	599	every	201
add	203	being	296	certain	395	desert	785	everyone	644
addition	822	believe	523	chance	916	design	714	everything	624
adjective	947	bell	855	change	180	details	984	exactly	695
afraid	944	belong	823	chart	933	determine	978	example	238
Africa	682	below	207	check	480	developed	540	except	836
after	116	beside	576	chief	869	dictionary	650	exciting	849
afternoon	300	best	338	child	784	did	94	exercise	534
again	179	better	337	children	252	didn't	322	expect	837
against	368	between	205	choose	767	died	693	experience	957
age	652	big	158	church	925	difference	542	experiment	737
ago	449	bill	506	circle	498	different	171	explain	464
agreed	930	birds	312	city	217	difficult	971	express	746
ahead	915	bit	770	class	433	direct	781	eye	219
air	184	black	342	clean	768	direction	510	face	279
all	34	block	896	clear	472	discovered	573	fact	423
allow	959	blood	852	climbed	704	distance	543	factories	906
almost	284	blow	843	close	232	divided	515	factors	611
alone	739	blue	537	clothes	594	division	997	fair	912
along	230	board	816	cloud	730	do	47	fall	389
already	626	boat	456	coast	763	doctor	809	family	298
also	145	body	301	cold	381	does	153	famous	844
although	656	bones	814	color	303	doesn't	974	far	281
always	241	book	269	column	923	dog	310	farm	376
am	482	born	917	come	96	dollars	866	farmers	512
America	198	both	243	common	462	done	401	fast	356
among	484	bottom	685	company	901	don't	227	father	212
amount	653	bought	965	compare	830	door	328	fear	960
an	43	box	408	complete	314	down	92	feel	422
and	3	boy	140	compound	818	draw	378	feeling	800
angle	680	branches	850	conditions	990	drawing	740	feet	254
animal	186	break	792	consider	858	dress	697	fell	777
another	154	bright	642	consonant	648	drive	600	felt	507
answer	192	bring	463	contain	427	drop	539	few	228
any	137	British	970	continued	707	dry	465	field	396
anything	514	broken	658	control	752	during	335	fig	948
appear	604	brother	562	cook	813	each	44	fight	690
apple	983	brought	459	cool	729	early	348	figure	394
are	15	brown	727	copy	631	ears	718	filled	476
area	308	build	669	corn	986	earth	218	finally	409
arms	561	building	431	corner	802	east	741	find	90
army	884	built	500	correct	411	easy	324	fine	496
around	146	burning	713	cost	788	eat	278	fingers	700
arrived	993	business	790	cotton	982	edge	568	finished	572
art	799	but	31	could	79	effect	998	fire	399
as	16	buy	621	couldn't	699	eggs	535	first	83
ask	165	by	29	count	672	eight	874	fish	307
at	21	call	86	country	208	either	607	fit	821
away	185	came	142	course	428	electric	803	five	361
baby	620	can	39	covered	355	elements	834	flat	838
back	112	cannot	487	cows	991	else	709	floor	617
bad	735	can't	501	create	969	end	152	flow	795
ball	492	capital	905	cried	382	energy	517	flowers	595
bank	764	captain	780	crops	805	engine	738	fly	406
base	448	car	255	cross	601	England	712	follow	141
be	22	care	616	crowd	831	English	402	food	204
bear	677	carefully	437	current	890	enjoy	833	foot	716
beat	694	carry	266	cut	290	enough	277	for	13
beautiful	565	case	635	dance	524	entered	862	force	458
became	415	cat	673	dark	491	entire	985	forest	549

word	#	word	#	word	#	word	#
form	147	history	787	lay	582	molecules	920	pair	497
forward	955	hit	807	lead	643	moment	659	paper	244
found	193	hold	358	learn	196	money	374	paragraph	589
four	265	hole	687	least	702	months	588	park	891
fraction	681	home	172	leave	297	moon	520	part	99
France	921	hope	633	led	966	more	72	particular	887
free	632	horse	311	left	226	morning	363	party	759
French	692	hot	479	legs	551	most	114	passed	364
fresh	937	hours	341	length	557	mother	191	past	569
friends	323	house	187	less	446	mountain	289	pattern	369
from	25	how	48	let	285	mouth	747	pay	742
front	421	however	339	let's	689	move	174	people	80
fruit	863	huge	950	letter	190	movement	847	per	657
full	478	human	798	level	918	much	130	perhaps	505
fun	856	hundred	367	lie	853	music	302	period	765
game	457	hunting	794	life	240	must	157	person	414
garden	773	I	20	lifted	882	my	81	phrase	628
gas	711	ice	608	light	220	name	120	picked	526
gave	407	idea	276	like	65	nation	637	picture	178
general	516	if	50	line	132	natural	665	piece	319
get	95	I'll	392	list	294	near	202	place	108
girl	287	important	250	listen	351	necessary	879	plains	710
give	113	in	6	little	105	need	169	plan	383
glass	579	inches	424	live	110	never	215	plane	451
go	74	include	499	located	994	new	101	planets	872
God	779	increase	786	long	91	next	235	plant	209
gold	662	Indian	282	look	70	night	257	play	182
gone	577	indicate	835	lost	731	no	77	please	774
good	121	industry	894	lot	666	nor	980	plural	928
got	246	information	745	loud	857	north	372	poem	832
government	475	insects	804	love	531	northern	968	point	188
grass	719	inside	439	low	340	nose	943	pole	848
great	126	instead	627	machine	447	not	32	poor	688
Greek	963	instruments	585	made	97	note	434	position	861
green	442	interest	560	main	553	nothing	435	possible	661
grew	721	interesting	840	major	876	notice	384	pounds	655
ground	388	into	67	make	64	noun	485	power	486
group	247	iron	698	man	123	now	89	practice	753
grow	262	is	7	many	56	number	76	prepared	934
guess	826	island	444	map	375	numeral	370	present	564
gun	951	isn't	909	march	967	object	481	president	726
had	28	it	10	mark	309	observe	877	pretty	935
hair	651	it's	299	match	972	ocean	432	printed	913
half	404	itself	708	material	493	of	2	probably	550
hand	177	Japanese	870	matter	502	off	181	problem	313
happened	344	job	567	may	98	office	949	process	883
happy	575	joined	715	maybe	789	often	248	produce	430
hard	236	jumped	613	me	111	oh	412	products	343
has	69	just	119	mean	135	oil	88	property	886
hat	885	keep	213	measure	346	old	136	provide	810
have	24	kept	559	meat	881	on	14	pulled	377
he	11	key	725	meet	586	once	268	pushed	619
head	222	killed	683	melody	684	one	27	put	151
hear	270	kind	176	members	525	only	104	questions	306
heard	325	king	390	men	167	open	237	quickly	413
heart	544	knew	316	metal	605	opposite	931	quiet	664
heat	477	know	107	method	645	or	26	quite	638
heavy	495	known	443	middle	670	order	326	race	563
held	598	lady	796	might	231	other	53	radio	902
help	128	lake	647	mile	256	our	118	rain	533
her	62	land	170	milk	663	out	55	raised	590
here	163	language	467	million	580	outside	623	ran	454
high	200	large	156	mind	530	over	100	rather	829
hill	618	last	210	mine	819	own	206	reached	350
him	66	late	274	minutes	419	oxygen	927	read	168
himself	359	laughed	636	miss	275	page	189	ready	513
his	18	law	717	modern	817	paint	529	real	283

word	#	word	#	word	#	word	#	word	#
reason	558	she	46	stone	667	thus	811	we	36
received	772	ship	332	stood	450	tied	864	wear	734
record	571	shoes	941	stop	271	time	68	weather	583
red	327	shop	938	store	566	tiny	660	week	445
region	521	short	336	story	224	to	5	weight	880
remain	696	should	197	straight	755	today	334	well	155
remember	347	shoulder	893	strange	775	together	245	we'll	903
repeated	922	shouted	706	stream	871	told	320	went	166
report	754	show	144	street	425	tone	806	were	35
represent	591	shown	416	stretched	956	too	134	west	581
rest	436	side	253	string	842	took	263	western	924
result	612	sight	868	strong	418	tools	989	what	33
return	522	sign	570	students	797	top	331	wheels	440
rhythm	873	silent	827	study	194	total	976	when	37
rich	865	similar	952	subject	518	touch	744	where	127
ride	615	simple	527	substances	987	toward	360	whether	593
right	133	since	317	such	160	town	391	which	45
ring	782	sing	386	suddenly	508	track	992	while	229
rise	756	single	743	suffix	939	trade	828	white	259
river	264	sir	995	sugar	946	train	536	who	87
road	403	sister	926	suggested	859	travel	397	whole	345
rock	353	sit	545	sum	546	tree	214	whose	771
rolled	676	six	489	summer	547	triangle	919	why	164
room	315	size	490	sun	305	trip	686	wide	555
root	584	skin	722	supply	801	trouble	728	wife	899
rope	981	sky	578	suppose	761	truck	911	wild	574
rose	958	sleep	609	sure	329	true	366	will	51
round	455	slowly	373	surface	429	try	175	win	973
row	701	small	149	surprise	691	tube	878	wind	352
rule	483	smell	988	swim	888	turn	162	window	541
run	249	smiled	679	syllables	504	two	71	wings	846
safe	824	snow	614	symbols	733	type	639	winter	554
said	40	so	60	system	452	uncle	793	wire	766
sail	675	soft	592	table	371	under	223	wish	538
same	138	soil	629	tail	815	underline	999	with	17
sand	808	soldiers	825	take	103	understand	460	within	649
sat	552	solution	936	talk	292	unit	393	without	272
save	736	solve	603	tall	625	until	251	woman	762
saw	225	some	61	teacher	597	up	52	women	964
say	125	someone	674	team	778	upon	400	wonder	678
scale	654	something	233	tell	139	us	173	won't	812
school	211	sometimes	288	temperature	641	use	42	wood	398
science	875	son	606	ten	405	usually	321	word	30
scientists	438	song	295	terms	889	valley	723	work	106
score	954	soon	293	test	509	value	845	workers	961
sea	260	sound	102	than	82	various	929	world	199
seat	996	south	385	that	9	verb	419	would	63
second	273	southern	910	the	1	very	115	wouldn't	914
section	646	space	354	their	49	view	1000	write	73
see	75	speak	602	them	58	village	610	written	556
seeds	760	special	494	themselves	640	visit	769	wrong	932
seem	234	speed	671	then	57	voice	379	wrote	705
seen	380	spell	183	there	41	vowel	365	yard	748
sell	892	spot	854	these	59	wait	410	year	109
send	867	spread	897	they	19	walk	258	yellow	908
sense	841	spring	634	thick	851	wall	548	yes	471
sent	732	square	503	thin	860	want	143	yet	474
sentence	122	stand	304	thing	117	war	387	you	8
separate	791	stars	420	think	124	warm	461	young	291
serve	783	start	216	third	587	was	12	your	38
set	150	state	267	this	23	wash	895	you're	720
settled	907	statement	757	those	242	Washington	962	yourself	751
seven	839	stay	441	though	466	wasn't	820		
several	357	steel	975	thought	221	watch	280		
shall	596	step	362	thousands	470	water	84		
shape	468	stick	758	three	148	waves	349		
sharp	900	still	195	through	129	way	78		

TESTING THE INSTANT WORDS _____

Beginning readers who are just learning to read, or those who have failed to learn to read properly from regular instruction, frequently have spotty reading vocabularies. They know some relatively uncommon words but do not know some of the words that appear most frequently.

Traditional basic reading textbooks have a graded word list built into the series. Many students, however, may not have followed a basic reading series or may have learned only part of the list. If so, it is important to "find out where the learner is."

To do this with individual students is easy. Give students the Instant Word Test on pages 44–45 or simply ask them to read aloud from each column of the Instant Words. Then stop and teach them the words they don't know.

In a group setting, a good way to assess word knowledge for beginning readers is to make a recognition test. Duplicate a group of Instant Words, four words per line, and number the lines. Give each student a sheet of the words and then say, "On line one, put an X on the word *you;* on line two, put an X on the word *that,*" and so on.

By correcting the tests, teachers can easily sort pupils into groups by ability. The tests can be saved for later student study or word review.

Instead of using this Survey Test, teachers may simply have students read every word on the Instant Word pages—but not all at once. Have them learn a page or part of a page at each lesson, until they have accumulated enough unfamiliar words for the day's lesson.

DIRECTIONS FOR THE INSTANT WORD TEST

The Instant Word Test is located on the next page. Ask individual students to read each word aloud slowly. Use a copy of the Instant Word Test for scoring, placing an *X* next to each word read incorrectly or omitted. Allow for dialect differences but accept only meaningful pronunciations. Do not give the student any help; if the student does not know a word after five seconds, tell him or her to go on to the next word.

Discontinue the exam when a student misses five words, not necessarily in consecutive order. Find the last correct word before the fifth error and multiply its position number by 15 to get the student's *approximate* instructional placement.

Because it is not standardized, the test does not yield a grade level score. It can, however, be used to determine where to begin working with a student on the 1000 Instant Words list. Do not use the test for teaching; instead use the complete list of Instant Words.

INSTANT WORD TEST _____

Student's Name _____

Examiner _____

Date _____ Class _____

Directions: Student reads aloud from one copy and examiner marks another copy. Stop after the student misses any five words. Do not help the student. If the student makes an error or hesitates five seconds or longer, say, "Try the next word."

Scoring:

(   ) Position number of last correct word before the fifth word missed

×   15

(   ) Approximate placement on the 1000 Instant Words list

For example, if the last correct word was tenth on the list below, then 10 × 15 = 150. You would then start teaching the Instant Words with word 151.

Test for the First 300 Words
(approximately every fifteenth word
in the first 300 words)

Test for the Second 300 Words
(approximately every fifteenth word
in the second 300 words)

1. are	21. room
2. but	22. become
3. which	23. whole
4. so	24. toward
5. see	25. map
6. now	26. king
7. only	27. certain
8. just	28. stars
9. too	29. nothing
10. small	30. stood
11. why	31. bring
12. again	32. check
13. study	33. heavy
14. last	34. direction
15. story	35. picked
16. beginning	36. window
17. feet	37. wide
18. book	38. sign
19. almost	39. root
20. family	40. describe

Test for the Next 400 Words
(approximately every fifteenth word in the next 400 words)

41.	ride	54.	provide
42.	bed	55.	guess
43.	lake	56.	interesting
44.	tiny	57.	bell
45.	sail	58.	chief
46.	fight	59.	army
47.	wrote	60.	sharp
48.	grew	61.	chance
49.	save	62.	agreed
50.	equal	63.	dead
51.	choose	64.	fear
52.	direct	65.	total
53.	flow	66.	conditions

Teaching the Instant Words

Since a high percentage of all reading material is composed of relatively few words, learning to read would appear to be a task that is ridiculously easy. If 300 words will do most of the job, why not begin with just these words, teach them quickly, and move on to the next level? The answer is that the learning experience is more complex than that.

Experience has shown that mastery of the first 300 Instant Words, or any basic vocabulary list of this size, normally takes about three years for beginning readers. An average student in an average learning situation knows most of the first 100 words toward the end of the first year of instruction. The second hundred words are added during the second year. It is not until some time in the third year that all 300 words are really mastered and used as part of the student's own reading vocabulary. This is not to deny that students at the second and third grade reading levels can "read" many more words than the 300 Instant Words. They can also read many proper nouns and a smattering of subject words related to the type of material that they have encountered.

Teachers can expect to decrease the learning time required to teach adult students in remedial reading classes. Nevertheless, students' mastery of the first 300 Instant Words closely parallels the reading level attained thus far. For example, a person who can just manage to read material at the upper-second-grade reading level barely knows most of the first 200 Instant Words.

It is important that beginning students learn most of the first 300 Instant Words. The remaining 700 of the 1,000 words are for reading and spelling lessons with students at about the fourth- and fifth-grade reading equivalency level.

Methods for teaching the Instant Words will vary with the teacher, the student, and the learning situation. Any method that works is a good one. Note that the Instant Words are presented in groups of five to discourage instructors from teaching too many words at once. Some students can learn only two or three words per week, and others can easily master twenty. Both groups need frequent word review.

Suggested activities include easy reading practice and using flash cards, card games, and spelling lessons augmented by a lot of praise and encouragement. Activities that also involve competition are fun and can enhance learning. Whether teaching students one-on-one or in a group setting, the important message for teachers to convey to students, by both word and deed, is that they care about them, that they want them to be able to read, and that learning these Instant Words is important.

TEACHING THE INSTANT WORDS _____

Easy Reading Practice

Easy reading practice is one of the best ways of teaching the Instant Words. For students who can read at the second-grade equivalency level, whether with help or hesitatingly, "easy reading" is reading first-grade level materials. *Easy reading material* is printed matter in which a student can pronounce 99 percent of the words, or material in which a student averages fewer than one mistake for every twenty words. Easy reading practice is especially beneficial because the material is certain to contain the Instant Words, and students who barely know these words get practice in recognizing them. Easy reading practice also helps students learn to apply context clues. Each reading gives them a feeling of success and encourages them to try to learn more words.

Easy reading, therefore, is reading that is a grade or two below where the student *can* read. If a student can read at the sixth-grade equivalency level, easy reading for that student is material at the fourth- or fifth-grade reading level. It is no accident that most popular novels are written at about the eighth-grade difficulty level and that most book buyers are at least high school graduates.

Flash Cards

Many teachers, tutors, and parents use flash cards to help teach sight word reading. A *flash card* is simply a card with a word written on it. The word is written in bold print and, usually, in lowercase using a marker or dark crayon. By cutting off the upper right hand corner of the card, the printed word will always be right side up and facing the person who restacks the cards.

she   **said**

A traditional way to teach using flash cards is to select a small number of words, such as five Instant Words. Tell the student each word and briefly discuss it, perhaps using it in an oral sentence. Next, mix up the cards and "flash" them to the student while he or she tries to quickly call out the word. If the student misses, give the word but don't use phonics at this point. Mix up the words and flash them to the student again. When the student knows all the words, put the cards away, and, at the next lesson, review the words by flashing the cards again. Help the student with any words missed.

TEACHING THE INSTANT WORDS

Flash cards also make great review lessons, and students often require considerable review of words learned. Just because they have mastered the list one day doesn't necessarily mean that students will remember all of the words the following week. Instead of blaming students for forgetting, praise them for any words remembered and patiently teach the words missed. Everyone needs repetition in learning people's names, in learning new words about a particular business, or in learning a new subject.

It is also a good idea to display flash cards for referral at times other than during the class period itself. Teachers can line them up on the chalkboard, and tutors might give a small stack of cards to a student to practice at home.

Flash cards are also effective sentence builders. Arrange two, three, or several flash cards so that they make a phrase or sentence. Some interesting sentences can be made using rebuses. A *rebus* is simply a picture used in place of a word, as in the following example:

The  hit the  .

Read this as "The man hit the dog."

In a game, the teacher can use flash cards with a small group of students, flashing each word as quickly as possible. The student who says the word first gets to keep the card. The point of the game is to see who gets the most cards. Give each student a turn at recognizing the word; when one student misses, the next one gets the turn.

Students sometimes work alone with a small pack of flash cards, separating them into two piles: the cards they know and those they do not know. When the students are finished, the teacher or a student who knows the words checks the "know" pile and then helps individual students with the "don't know" pile.

A teacher or tutor can make flash cards from blank calling cards obtained from a printer, on index cards, or on scraps of paper. Copy the entire word list to be learned or make cards only for the words that students miss when reading down the list. Students can even make their own flash cards.

Remember that teaching only a few words at a time keeps the student's success rate high.

TEACHING THE INSTANT WORDS _____

Bingo Game

Bingo is an excellent game for teaching the Instant Words in a group setting or one-on-one. Twenty-five words (in five rows and five columns) are placed in random order on a card, with a card for each student who plays. Each player's card contains the same words but arranged in a different order. The teacher or tutor calls off the words in random order or draws word cards out of a hat. Markers can be small cardboard squares, bottle caps, beans, or anything handy. The first student to complete a row, column, or diagonal line wins.

Even after there has been a winner, students often like to continue playing until the cards are filled and every word is covered. Playing the game this way helps the teacher spot poor readers by observing the number of uncovered words on students' cards. A situation in which some of the students do not know all of the words is a great opportunity for the teacher to write an unfamiliar word on the board after saying it. Playing until all cards are covered also gives poor readers an equal chance at winning, which is always desirable.

Note that a set of twenty-five words will fit on a card with five rows and five columns. For beginning readers, however, having just nine words (in three rows and three columns) on a card may be enough.

Sample Bingo Card

the	of	it	with	at
a	can	on	are	this
is	will	you	to	and
your	that	we	as	but
be	in	not	for	have

Teaching the Instant Words _____

Pairs Game

Another game played with great success is called *Pairs*. Pairs is played like rummy or fish in that only two cards are needed to make a pair. Two to five persons may play. Five word cards are dealt to each player, and the remainder of the deck is placed in the center of the table.

The object of the game is to get as many pairs as possible. Each deck has sets of two identical cards.

The player to the right of the dealer may ask any other player for a specific card, for example, "Do you have *and?*" The player who asks must hold the mate to the *and* card. The player who is asked must give up the card if he holds it. If the first player does not get the card he asks for, he draws a card from the pile. Then the next player takes a turn to ask for a card.

If the player succeeds in getting the card he asks for, either from another player or from the pile, he gets another turn. As soon as the player gets a pair, he puts it down in front of him. The player with the most pairs at the end of the game wins.

If the player *doing the asking* does not know how to read the word on the card, he may show the card and ask any of the other players or anyone present.

If the player *who is asked* for a card does not know how to read that word or is unsure of the word, he should ask to see the card of the player requesting the card or ask a nonplaying person who can read to look at his hand.

Make two cards for each word used in a Pairs *deck.*

TEACHING THE INSTANT WORDS _____

Use a group of twenty-five Instant Words to make the word cards for the decks. Two cards for each word makes a fifty-card deck. Teachers or students themselves can make the cards, which should contain words at the appropriate level of difficulty for the students. Although it is good for students to periodically review easy words already mastered, instructional games should generally follow the same rules as those used to select instructional reading material—not too easy and not too hard. The students, therefore, should know some but not all of the words used in a particular deck. They should have help in playing until they know almost all of the words and can get along by themselves. This level of mastery is usually attained quickly because the game is highly motivating.

The students should play the game on several occasions until they can call out all the words instantly. They should then progress to a deck of word cards at the next level of difficulty, periodically reviewing easier decks.

Concentration

A Pairs deck can also be used to play a kind of Concentration™ game. Spread a deck of fifty cards facedown on a table in mixed order. One to four players by turns draws two cards at random. If the cards drawn are not a pair, the player puts them back in exactly the same place, facedown. The trick of the game is to remember card location in order to make a pair with each two cards turned up. From an instructional standpoint, the student gets practice in reading aloud each card turned over. If that player doesn't know how to read the card, another player can help by saying the words.

SPELLING

The Instant Words may be used for spelling lessons, especially those words that students have trouble learning to read. However, the Instant Words are just as important for student writing as they are for reading because students need the basic words, such as *and, is,* and *to,* that hold sentences together. Here is a specific method instructors can use to teach spelling.

1. **Use the test-study method** by first giving students a spelling test of twenty Instant Words.

   1a. Have the students correct their own papers. During the first few classes in which you use the test-study method, check students' papers to see that they have found the words they misspelled and have spelled them correctly. After a relatively short while, most students can do the self-correcting satisfactorily; however, a few students may need frequent or continual supervision.

   1b. Have the students carefully study the words they missed, paying careful attention to just the incorrect or missing letters, perhaps by circling the incorrect letter(s) and writing the word correctly from memory several times. See also the Five-Step Study Method following this section.

2. **Give a second spelling test.** Students who get either 100 percent or perhaps 90 percent of the words correct will not have to take the test again.

3. **Give a final test** to only those students who did not do well on the previous test. They should study just the words and letters they missed. Instructors can help the students by going over phonics, syllabication, spelling patterns, principles of forming suffixes, or irregular spellings.

4. **Students can keep a chart of final scores** achieved on their final spelling tests.

It is important to avoid presenting too many words in a spelling lesson. Five to ten words for a student reading at the first-grade equivalency level and twenty words for those at reading levels three to six are probably enough.

PELLING

Five-Step Study Method for Students

1. **Look** at the whole word carefully.

2. **Say** the word aloud to yourself.

3. **Spell** each letter aloud to yourself.

4. **Write** the word from memory. (Cover the word and write it.)

5. **Check** your written word against the correct spelling. (Circle errors and repeat Steps 4 and 5.)

PICTURE NOUNS

This section contains 100 words intended to supplement the Instant Words. *Picture nouns* are easily pictured words that students need when writing stories. The list of Instant Words does not contain many "subject words," or words that describe content.

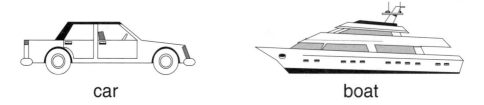

car   boat

A group of five picture nouns can be taught along with the Instant Words, which are also presented in groups of five words at a time. They are particularly useful when using flash cards as sentence builders because the picture side of the card can be used as a rebus.

Picture nouns can also be used to strengthen thinking skills. Mix up two or more groups of five picture nouns and have students sort them into piles that belong together. This activity makes students organize like words into categories, and it gives them practice reading words.

Another way to teach picture nouns is to make a set of flash cards for the number of words to be presented. Just put the printed word on one side of a card and the picture for that word on the other.

The picture nouns can also be used in self-teaching lessons. Give the student a stack of cards with the word side facing up. The student tries to read the word, and if she can't, she turns the card over to look at the picture.

Most of the games and techniques used in teaching the Instant Words can also be used with the picture nouns.

Picture Nouns

Group 1

boy

girl

man

woman

baby

Group 2

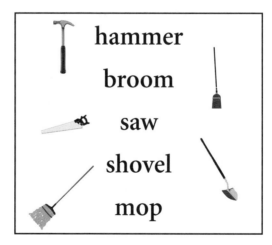

hammer

broom

saw

shovel

mop

Group 3

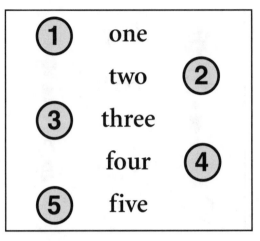

Group 4

Picture Nouns

Group 5

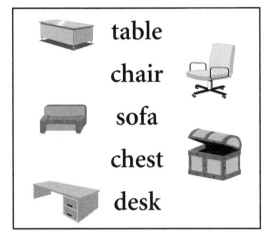

table

chair

sofa

chest

desk

Group 6

cat

dog

bird

fish

rabbit

Group 7

Group 8

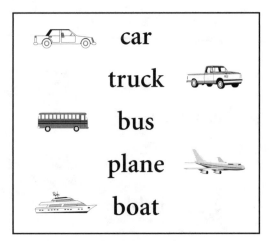

Group 9

bread

meat

soup

egg

salad

Group 10

water

milk

juice

soda

tea

Group 11

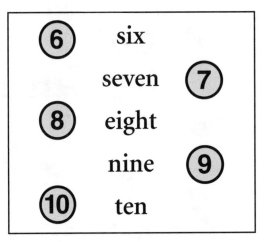

6 six		
	seven	**7**
8 eight		
	nine	**9**
10 ten		

Group 12

cherries

orange

grapes

pear

banana

Picture Nouns

Group 13

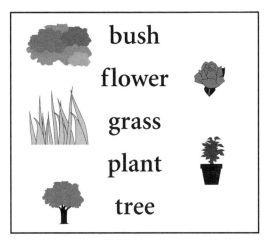

bush

flower

grass

plant

tree

Group 14

sun

moon

star

cloud

rain

Group 15

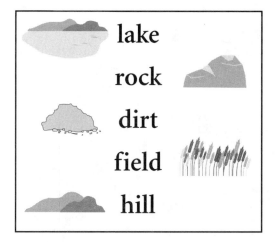

Group 16

PICTURE NOUNS

Group 17

farmer

police

cook

doctor

teacher

Group 18

television

radio

movie

ballplayer

band

Group 19

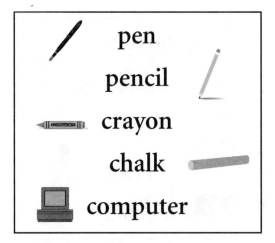

pen
pencil
crayon
chalk
computer

Group 20

book
newspaper
magazine
sign
letter